MW00912705

MANLY ADVENTURES

AND OTHER DELUSIONS

GRETCHEN,
MAY THESE STORIES
COME SOFTLY TO YOU
Tom Wilson

BY TOM WILSON

ILLUSTRATED BY DANNY SHAW

RED APPLE PUBLISHING

COPYRIGHT © 1995

SECOND EDITION 1998

ALL RIGHTS RESERVED. NO PART OF THIS BOOK MAY BE
REPRODUCED OR TRANSMITTED IN ANY FORM OR BY ANY
MEANS, ELECTRONIC OR MECHANICAL, INCLUDING
PHOTOCOPYING, RECORDING OR BY ANY INFORMATION
STORAGE AND RETRIEVAL SYSTEM, WITHOUT THE WRITTEN
PERMISSION OF WILSON-SHAW.

LIBRARY OF CONGRESS CATALOG NUMBER 95-70803

ISBN 1-880222-23-X

RED APPLE PUBLISHING
15010 113TH ST. KPN
GIG HARBOR, WA 98329

PRINTED BY GORHAM PRINTING
ROCHESTER, WA, 98579

PAGE AND COVER DESIGN (EXCEPT FOR ILLUSTRATION)
BY KATHRYN E. CAMPBELL

MANUFACTURED IN THE UNITED STATES OF AMERICA

IN MEMORY OF

David Cantlin

Contents

The Vest

CAMPING IS A MANLY THING TO DO. MANLY CAMPING can only happen when real men go to manly places outdoors and do manly things.

This is a story about one such manly camping trip. Roger, his wife Marlene, my wife Lynne and I left for a four-day trip up the South Fork of the Hoh River. Roger and I wanted to build a manly camp out of mud, rocks, sticks and brush, but the wives made us take the stupid ol' camper. That was okay though 'cause there were plenty of other manly things for Roger and me to do. We would spend that first evening preparing to head out bright and early the next morning to hunt down and capture many killer steelhead trout.

Few things are manlier than facing the flesh-tearing teeth of one of those ten-pound river monsters armed with nothing but a flimsy graphite stick and the manly will to survive.

I've always looked at steelhead hunting as the ultimate test of manliness. After all, when your rod tip bends with the power of one of those frightening creatures, you gotta figure that it's either him or you.

That evening Roger and I decided to start a fire the manly way by rubbing two sticks together. We would have done it too if it hadn't a been for our arms getting tired.

We sat by the fire, that Lynne and Marlene had started, and dreamed of the manly adventures we would experience in the days to come.

"Hey, Roger," I mumbled, "wait till you see what I got." I walked over to the car and carefully lifted the rectangular cardboard box from its place of honor in the trunk.

Roger and I trembled with manly anticipation as I peeled back the box flaps to unveil the ultimate in manly attire—a camouflage-colored, multi-pocked, velcro-closured, water-resistant steelhead vest with double-stitched, back-mounted fish pocket, and genuine lamb's wool hook patch.

Roger and I fell silent with manly respect as I lifted my masterpiece skyward. Silhouetted against the evening light, it appeared to us as a warrior's shield of honor. Our silent reverence was suddenly and rudely interrupted by the

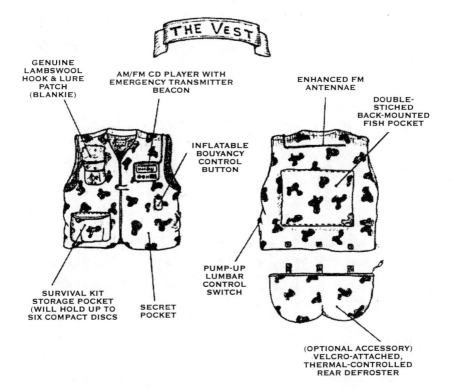

THE VEST

GENUINE LAMBSWOOL HOOK & LURE PATCH (BLANKIE)

AM/FM CD PLAYER WITH EMERGENCY TRANSMITTER BEACON

ENHANCED FM ANTENNAE

DOUBLE-STICHED BACK-MOUNTED FISH POCKET

INFLATABLE BOUYANCY CONTROL BUTTON

PUMP-UP LUMBAR CONTROL SWITCH

SURVIVAL KIT STORAGE POCKET (WILL HOLD UP TO SIX COMPACT DISCS

SECRET POCKET

(OPTIONAL ACCESSORY) VELCRO-ATTACHED, THERMAL-CONTROLLED REAR DEFROSTER

inquisitive women.

"Hey, what's that little square patch of wool for over the left front pocket?" asked Marlene. I was overcome by a manly sense of pride. The little woman wanted to know what the manly patch of wool was for.

"That's for hooking my dangerously sharp, steelhead-killing flies and lures on," I proudly explained.

"Oh sure," was the sarcastic reply from Lynne. "Looks more like a piece of your blankie to me."

I find it amazing how fragile manliness can be. One well-timed, sarcastic comment from virtually any woman can instantly strip away the thin veneer of any man's manliness.

The next day Roger and I, hunting knives strapped to

our belts, set out through the wild animal-infested forest on our dangerous quest for the killer steelhead. The wives, in spite of our repeated warnings of potential wilderness peril, decided to follow along and pick berries and wild flowers.

Roger and I finally reached the river. We spent several manly minutes investigating animal droppings to ascertain if any imminent danger existed. Roger explained how he didn't think it was necessary for me to check dropping freshness and temperature by inserting my index finger.

We surveyed the terrain and determined that it was imperative that we cross the river. Crossing roaring, man-killing rapids, as all men know, is a manly endeavor. Roger and I staged our bodies perpendicular to the river's current. We interlocked our arms in a manly death grip, hand to wrist, and painstakingly struggled, step by agonizing step, across the raging torrent. We reached the other side, out of breath and exhausted from our manly experience, only to find our wives sitting on a log smiling down at us.

"How did you gals get over here?" Roger queried.

"We crossed on that log over there, dear," said Marlene, sarcastically, while she mockingly batted her eyelashes. "Did you guys have fun holding hands crossing the river?"

I find it amazing how fragile manliness can be. One well-timed, sarcastic comment from virtually any woman can instantly strip away the thin veneer of any man's manliness.

That night back at camp Roger and I were subdued. I gazed over at Roger—his face reflected the depth and sadness of our common tragedy. Here we were, two manly shells of our former manliness, egos crushed and stripped of our pride, sulking and pouting by the fire.

"I must do something," I thought to myself. "This lack of manliness is unbearable!"

Then it happened. A spark of genius welled up inside me. "Hey, Roger, let's go cut down a tree!"

Roger's face lit up. "I'll get my chainsaw!" he exclaimed. Few items are manlier than a chainsaw. Roger and I were strapping on our knives when Lynne's voice suddenly shattered the evening air.

"Tom," she ordered, "the only thing you guys are going to cut down to size is this three-foot-high pile of dirty dishes. It's your turn to wash."

I find it amazing how fragile manliness can be. One well-timed, sarcastic comment from virtually any woman can instantly strip away the thin veneer of any man's manliness.

Dances With Snakes

THE YEAR WAS NINETEEN-HUNDRED-FIFTY-FIVE. I WAS five, my big sister, Patty, was ten, and she was my hero. She could run faster, climb higher, swim farther and catch more snakes and lizards than anyone else in the neighborhood.

Some of the kids called her *Animal Woman*. If a wounded, lost, or abandoned fish, bird, cat, dog, or reptile came anywhere near our house, her voluntary band of "trained paramedic" neighborhood kids would rescue it, pack it on a pillow in a Red Ryder wagon, and bring it to Animal Woman. Why she didn't become a veterinarian I'll never know.

I watched her feed baby birds with an eye dropper and fix their broken, little wings with popsicle sticks and adhesive tape. I watched her rub iodine on everything from punctured puppy paws to traumatized tabby tails. She was an artist as she painted Mercurochrome masterpieces on fractured fish fins and lacerated lizard lips.

This is a story about her most famous fix. This modern medical miracle would have surely made her a prime candidate for the Mother Teresa/Clara Barton Humanitarian Award for Animal Women, if such a prize had existed.

It was early afternoon on a hot, humid, summer day. Patty and I were in the backyard watching baby lizards hatch from their jelly-like egg sacks. One of the "trained paramedic" neighborhood kids pulled up in a red wagon with a wounded snake curled in the center of the pillow.

"This poor creature must be in excruciating pain!" Patty exclaimed. "It has a quarter-inch-long gash on its underside!"

Animal Woman never panicked. She calmly sprayed the wound with Bactine and, with the skill of a trained physician, tightly bound the laceration with adhesive tape.

This medical emergency was only a hint of what was to come. The following day two more wagons with two more snakes were brought in with the same wound. Three more were transported the day after that. It was all too clear that some sort of deadly, reptilian, skin-splitting, possibly extinction-threatening epidemic was running rampant through the neighborhood. Animal Woman never quavered. She single-handedly washed, sprayed, bandaged and released thirty-one snakes.

I remember Patty and me sitting on the couch. Animal Woman was upset and I was confused because our mother, clearly trying to suppress her laughter, was projecting a total lack of empathy for the poor wounded creatures. She attempted to explain the biology of the situation in her best parental terms.

"You see kids…ah…what goes in a snake has gotta come out…I mean…ah…you know…when ya eat, ya gotta go and when ya gotta go, ya gotta go." It was clumsy but we understood.

To this very day I have a mind's-eye vision of thirty-one snakes with bodies bloated and little snake eyes bugging out, twisting, contorting and slithering around in a reptilian panic. My mother's words and wisdom are still fresh in my memory, and the older I get the more I understand that "When ya gotta go, ya gotta go."

Charlie's Treasure

RUMORS OF BURIED TREASURE HAVE FASCINATED AND tempted mankind for centuries. One such rumor concerned the burial of a large sum of gold in the hills around Seabeck, Washington. One such fascinated and tempted man was none other than Charlie.

Charlie had checked out the book *Lost Treasures of the Northwest* from the library. On a clear, cool Sunday morning in 1980, Charlie, book and shovel in hand, armed with a state-of-the-art, ultra-high-tech, metal detector and young son in tow, struck out into the hills to find his fortune.

They had traveled barely one-hundred yards when the electronic alarm sent chills of excitement up and down his spine while his mind flashed on visions of riches and early retirement.

"We've hit the big one, Son!" he screeched. "This is it, the lost treasure of Seabeck!" A quick pass of the metal detector over the hole and a clump of overturned earth revealed nothing. "It's okay, Kid, there're plenty of places to look and plenty of holes to dig," Charlie said with confidence.

Time after time the squeal of the detector fueled a furious dig for wealth. Time after time the overturned earth revealed nothing. Charlie's frustration was mounting. "This thing's got to be broke," he thought to himself.

Ten hours passed. Twenty-five holes were dug. The lowering sun cast eerie shadows on the forest floor. No treasures, no riches, no early retirement. "Let's go home, Son. We can try again another day."

As they walked back to the car, Charlie's young son gazed up at him, and with one innocent remark solved the mystery of the squealing metal detector. "Hey, Dad, how come you're wearing your steel-toed boots when you ain't at work?"

The Great
Bavarian Bovine Battle

DAN WAS FRESH OUT OF BOOT CAMP AND STATIONED IN Germany. He was assigned to an Advanced Scout Squad under Corporal Eddie Bristow. Their mission was to participate in joint U.S. and Canadian maneuvers.

Few things are manlier than an eighteen-year-old boy in full battle gear—M16 rifle with attached M203 grenade launcher and multiple clips, Army-issue knife with black leather handle and curved serrated blade, bloused field pants, full pack, taped buckles for silent running, and camouflage face paint.

Corporal Bristow had gathered Dan and the rest of the troops by a wooden fence at the edge of a large field next to an old German farmhouse.

"Listen up, men!" he ordered. "It is now zero eight hundred hours. At zero eight-o-three we climb the fence, form a five-meter spread formation to minimize grenade casualties, and conduct phase 1, Enemy Search and..."

Corporal Bristow's orders were interrupted by the sweet voice of a thirteen-year-old German farm girl who had stealthily flounced up from behind. She cooed, "What's that green and black stuff on your face?"

Corporal Bristow cleared his throat and replied in a manly voice which suddenly seemed several octaves lower than normal. "This is government issue, regulation, camouflage face paint, ma'am."

The young girl smiled. "It looks like makeup to me," she said as she pirouetted on one foot and swished away, her skirt twirling in the breeze.

I find it amazing how fragile manliness can be. One well-timed, sarcastic comment from virtually any woman can instantly strip away the thin veneer of any man's manliness.

Corporal Bristow cleared his throat and wiped the sudden perspiration from his face. He looked down at his watch and, in a cracking pubescent voice, sputtered the command, "Zero eight-o-three, men. Let's head out." Dan and the other brave men of the Advanced Scout Squad under Corporal Eddie Bristow climbed the fence, assumed a five-meter spread and moved stealthily forward toward the center of the meadow.

Dan's eyes surveyed the subtle contours of the rolling field, but his mind drifted back to his hometown. He could almost smell the flowery fragrance of that cute little red-haired girl who worked at the fast-food joint on the corner of 6th and Main.

A sudden movement in the bushes off to his side startled him back to reality. "Corporal Bristow," he whispered, "we have possible enemy movement in the bushes off to the right."

Corporal Bristow, waving his hands wildly, ordered a flanking maneuver to surround and subdue. The boot camp training was evident on the faces of these brave men. These were killing machines—no fear, no hesitation. The signal of thumbs-up readiness was flashed as each man reached his position.

Corporal Bristow peered into the bushes with a snake-eyed stare and issued an ultimatum to the enemy, "Okay in there. Toss out your weapons and come out with your hands up!"

The bushes rustled. No weapons. No response.

"Toss out your weapons or else!" he commanded. The

bushes rustled. No weapons. No response.

Corporal Bristow gazed at his men and shrugged his shoulders. "This is going to require a little nudge," he thought to himself. He raised his M-16 in the air and fired one round.

All hell broke loose. The bushes parted and a dozen cows headed straight for the men of the Advanced Scout

Squad. "Run away, run away!" yelled Corporal Bristow. "Every man for himself!" Weapons, helmets, and backpacks flew in all directions. The rout was complete.

Dan surged forward, barely maintaining his balance. He could feel the moist, hay-laden breath of a vicious bovine on the back of his neck as he tumbled and stumbled toward the safety of the fence. Sanctuary was but a few feet away. The lethal beast seemed within inches.

Dan's thoughts raced back and forth from panic to visions of his loving parents standing face-to-face with a solemn uniformed messenger at the front door of the family home. "We're terribly sorry, sir, ma'am, but your handsome, talented, heroic, and incredibly manly son was trampled and eaten by a killer Communist cow while defending the country he loves." For a split second he flashed on the headlines in the local gazette: "Dan died a manly man—posthumously awarded Medal of Honor."

The sound of the snorting brute slurping at his heels brought him back to his senses. To this day Dan is unable to recall how he cleared the fence, but eyewitness reports have described a head-first, double-twist, with a half roll, reminiscent of the infamous Fosberg flop.

He lay there helpless, chest heaving, perspiration dripping from his forehead into his eyes. He had faced death and survived. For a split second he again flashed on the headlines in the local gazette back home: "Dan conquers killer cow—awarded Medal of Honor."

The voice of the young farm girl rudely intruded on the daydreaming smile that had contorted his mud-covered face.

"Sorry, G.I., did my Helga scare you?"

I find it amazing how fragile manliness can be. One well-timed, sarcastic comment from virtually any woman can instantly strip away the thin veneer of any man's manliness.

The Flight Into Infamy

THE ANNUAL COMPANY PICNIC WAS HELD AT TWANOH
State Park, August 1977. The big boss was flippin' burgers
while dozens of flying frisbees filled the air. It was a classic
Pacific Northwest August day—eighty-one degrees in the
shade and a light breeze out of the north. Down at the beach
the kids were splashing in the muddy brown wading pool
and the adults, nursing their favorite cool one, were fully
greased and sprawled all over the hot pebble beach.

The center of attention was Dale Fransen's hang-gliding
tow kite. This was not your modern, 1994 version, ultra-high-
tech para-sail. This was a circa 1976, nylon-covered, aluminum-framed, high-flying, man-eating death machine. All of
the macho men of the beach were gathered around, stomachs sucked to the backbone, jockeying for position.

Volunteers to *talk* about taking the initial flight into in-
famy were numerous. Complete idiots that would actually
attach themselves to this contraption numbered one—yours
truly.

Dale Fransen was a pro. He made it look easy. I had
watched him ascend on a five-hundred-foot rope till he
looked like a tiny dot against the blue sky. He would release

the rope and free himself from the boat, soar like an eagle for twenty minutes, and then gracefully ride a cushion of air to a pin-point landing and a standing ovation by a bikini- clad gaggle of admirers on the beach.

"Self," I said to myself, "I can do that." I was overcome by a Jacque Cousteau-like sense of adventure.

Friend Fransen, the consummate instructor, was in his glory. "Listen up, Tom. If you place your hands on the cross-bar about this far apart and push the bar out, the kite will rise, and if you pull the bar in, she'll dive." I listened intently to the prerequisite hour of intense instruction. Problem was, I was so busy sucking my stomach into my backbone I only remembered five minutes of it.

Strapped in the kite with my ski firmly attached, I assumed the sitting position. I couldn't help being temporarily distracted by the weird guttural sounds emanating from deep in my throat as various parts of my anatomy touched the cool canal water. My poor heart was pumping at one-eighty.

I attempted to firmly issue the "Hit it!" command. It came out sounding more like a question: "Hit it?"

At twenty knots I was skiing. Since I had skied before, I remember starting to feel pretty confident. A tenth of a second later I was forty feet in the air looking down. My body relieved itself. I whipped to the left and I whipped to the right. I was totally out of control and at the mercy of the wind and fate. My shoulders ached as the steering bar furiously attempted to rip my arms from my body.

Then it happened. For one brief moment in time I was in control. I was flying. Although it seemed like an hour, Dale

told me later it was between three and five seconds. In that moment of exultation, I was the conqueror. I had won and victory was indeed sweet.

I tried to look down at the tiny figures in the boat below, but my body was in the way. "No problem," I thought. "I'll just pull the bar toward me." Wrong! If you can imagine being catapulted off the end of an aircraft carrier straight into a brick wall with twenty pounds of metal and nylon kite strapped to your back, you probably have a good idea of what it felt like. It was the mother of all flights.

I went from forty feet high to zero in two-tenths of a second. You know how you skip across the surface of the

water when you fall while skiing? Can you recall that sense of exhilaration when your body finally digs in? Well, I didn't skip! My feet hit first. The flight of victory and the agony of da feet.

The rest of my body seemed to hit at the same time. I remember feeling the skin on my face stretch around the back of my head as my teeth fell in tiny pieces from my multiply-lacerated lips. All traces of life-giving oxygen were forced from my lungs, which was unfortunate because it seemed like it took at least two hours for my head to break the surface.

As I lay there, stunned and gasping for air, I swear I heard the theme from *Jaws*. I was thankful that there were no Great Whites in the canal because both of my shins were bleeding profusely.

To this day, I distinctly remember Dale's voice calmly expressing concern and encouragement. "Hey, is the kite okay? You wanna go back up?"

Other macho men of adventure sucked their stomachs to their backbones and tried the kite that summer. Some fared better than me; some fared far worse. But none who tried will forget their experience with Dale Fransen's circa 1976, nylon-covered, aluminum-framed, high-flying, man-eating death machine.

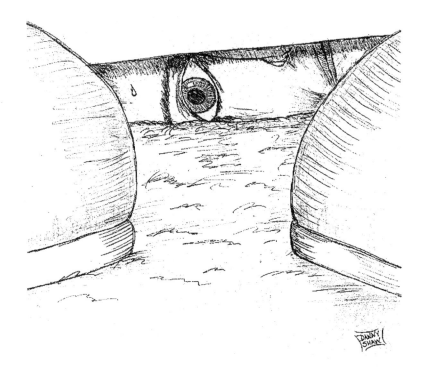

The Silent Sentinels

I DO NOT RECALL WHAT I SAID TO MY FATHER, BUT I DO remember him growling like a beast, leaping from his chair, and chasing me through the house. I was only eight years old, so I know, had he really wanted to, he could have caught me. I could feel his hands grabbing at my shirt in a mock attempt to snag his prey. I reached the bathroom, slammed the door, and pushed in the lock. I stood still for a minute, shaking from the rush of adrenaline that floods your body when you just barely make it to safety.

I held my breath, put my ear to the door, and listened for any indication of his presence. I could hear nothing. I rested my face on the cold tile, and peered through the tiny crack between the bottom of the door and the floor. I could see my father standing there patiently waiting for me to give up, come out, and be eaten alive.

I wasn't going to open that door as long as he was poised to pounce. Time after time I peeked through the crack under the door only to find my father still standing and waiting.

Two hours passed and the entire eight years of my life flashed before my eyes. Two hours is an eternity to a kid. "I'll die in here," I thought. "I've got to escape." My plan was to swing the door open, fly under his legs, and run for my life. I slowly wrapped my small hand around the door handle, took a deep breath, and pulled with all of my strength. There, on the carpet in front of the door, were my father's shoes.

St. Valentine's Day Garage Massacre

IT WAS LATE IN THE AFTERNOON ON THE EVENING OF February 14, 1989. Friend Rick was working on his 1978 SR5 long-bed Toyota pickup. He had removed the alternator, replaced the brushes, and had just completed reinstallation. The hard part was over.

Rick's face radiated a cocky confidence as he grabbed a clean rag, wiped the greasy residue from his hands, and slid into the driver's seat, right leg on the gas pedal, left leg out the door and on the pavement. The final test was all that remained. The charging circuit indicator light, which had been glowing bright red, needed only to fade out to indicate success.

Rick inserted the key. A satisfied smile crossed his face as the key was turned. But the smile was short-lived. Faster than you can say "Whoops," the now infamous St. Valentine's Day Garage Massacre began.

Rick's 1978 SR5 long-bed Toyota pickup was in gear! The truck lurched forward into the garage. Rick saved his left leg from a messy amputation by jerking it inside seconds before the truck door was slammed shut by the side of the garage entrance. The nose of the truck went under the front end of the elevated table saw, starting it up, and the whole mobile disaster headed for the back wall. Rick's over-forty reflexes finally directed his foot to the brake pedal, which he pushed with enthusiasm.

Regaining control of his bodily functions, he slowly glanced up at the table saw and was relieved to find that the blade was in the down position. He was about to take some comfort from the realization that his years of machine shop safety-awareness training were not a total loss when, out of the corner of his eye, he noticed the two-pound coffee can full of finishing nails tipping precariously on the edge of the saw table.

Rick's hand reached for the door handle. It was too late. The can and its contents, as if in slow motion, fell forward, landing on top of the radiator. A steady stream of finishing nails spilled onto the still-running fan blades, and the resulting machine-gun effect peppered the walls and ceiling of the garage with deadly projectiles.

The nails were finally exhausted. The neighborhood kids were gathering in the driveway. Rick sat silently in stunned disbelief. He took a deep breath and glanced down. A satisfied, if somewhat strained, smile crossed his face. The indicator light was out.

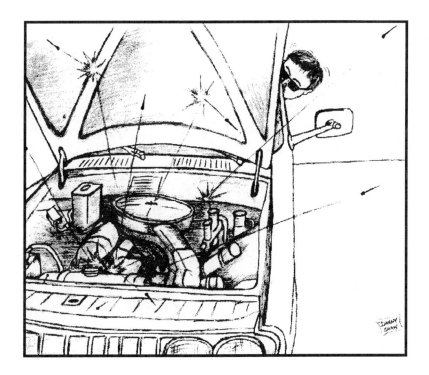

The Big Game

I WAS UP EARLY. I HAD A LARGE BREAKFAST OF EGGS, pancakes, toast, bacon and orange juice. The day of the big game had arrived. I had been cordially invited to strap on the pads, slip on the helmet, and partake in a manly game of tackle football. Tackle football is the ultimate manly adventure.

The wife's words of encouragement from the previous evening still echoed in my ears: "You're too old to play tackle football; you'll hurt yourself!" A man expects his wife to be supportive of his manly endeavors.

Besides, Kareem Abdul-Jabbar was running up and down the Great Western Forum when he was 42; Nolan Ryan was still tossin' fastballs at 45; and Jimmy Connors did very well in his last major tennis tournament, and he was no spring chicken!

I was a pretty good wide receiver in my youth, and I saw no reason why I shouldn't take advantage of this manly opportunity to capture some lost glory. I lifted my cleats from their longtime resting place on the basement wall. The leather had hardened and cracked, and there were cobwebs inside, but the cleats themselves were still firmly anchored

and would most certainly propel me to victory. They almost seemed to glow with a manly aura.

I stood in silence and cradled these dust-covered, battle-scarred remnants of an earlier age, as my mind drifted back to past moments of manly skirmishes on the chalk-lined gridiron.

My private, poignant moment of silent reverence was, however, short-lived as the wife's voice echoed through the heater duct. "Your friends are here, dear. How are you going to get up after they tackle you? It takes you ten minutes just to get up off the couch."

I find it amazing how fragile manliness can be. One well-timed, sarcastic comment from virtually any woman can instantly strip away the thin veneer of any man's manliness.

I arrived at the field a full twenty minutes before the scheduled kickoff. I strapped on my cleats, did my pre-game stretch, ran one half of a lap, and collapsed in a breathless heap. Captains were chosen and team members were selected. I was picked last, but that was okay, 'cause my slight paunch and graying temples were probably misleading to these younger, ill-informed, modern-day warriors and, besides, why should I be bothered by the obvious ignorance of a bunch of punks!

The rules were decided—short field, three complete passes for a first down, first team to score twice wins. My team won the toss and elected to receive.

The ball was kicked right into my waiting arms. My legs began churning as a rush of adrenaline surged through my body. My teammates used their bodies to form what appeared to be an impenetrable wall of blockers up the right side of the field.

There is no moment in a man's life that is manlier than the kickoff return. Kickoff returns are the epitome of manliness. Bodies, propelled by finely-tuned and powerful muscle

and sinew, fly in every direction making contact with each other at blinding rates of speed.

I ran around my wall of blockers and cut back into the center of the field. But, I failed to see the two defenders bearing down on me from behind. The impact of their bodies sent me spinning to the ground. Pain surged through my spine as the sheer force of their multiple blows drove my unpadded shoulder into the turf.

I lay there breathless as my attackers piled off my back. The pain in my shoulder was numbed by the realization of my accomplishment—a twenty-yard gain, first and ten! My teammates, in a manly display of admiration and male bonding, eloquently acknowledged my accomplishment.

"Nice run, Dude!" We held hands in the huddle in a manly sorta way, and the quarterback called out our first play from scrimmage.

"Okay, John, you do a down 'n' out, and, Ron, you run a post pattern, and you, Dude, block somebody and just go out somewhere."

I informed the guy that my name was Tom, not Dude, but he was obviously busy mentally preparing himself for the coming play and responded with, "Sure, Dude, whatever you say."

The line of scrimmage is most likely the manliest place on earth. Warriors poised in a three-point stance, face to face, man to man. Eyes glared across an imaginary line. Bodies, coiled like springs, waited to surge into combat.

The quarterback barked the signals: "Hut one, hut two, hike!" The ball was snapped, and I battled my way around my opponent. Time seemed to slow down. I cut to the left and I cut to the right. As I turned to face the quarterback, I found myself in the middle of a wide receiver's ultimate dream. I was all alone in the end zone.

I did the only manly thing I could do. I began jumping

up and down and waving my hands while wildly yelling, "I'm open, I'm open! Throw it here, throw it to me!"

I could almost hear the cheers of hundreds...no thousands...of screaming fans as I envisioned myself plucking the ball from its crescent trajectory and slamming it to the turf in a triumphant display of manly conquest. This would be for posterity. This would be the fifteen seconds of manly fame to which each man is entitled. This story would be told and retold, year after year, around countless campfires, for and by the children of my children. I closed my eyes and attempted to prolong the magnificence of the moment by imagining my teammates lifting me up on their shoulders in a glorious dance of victory.

However, the dream was rudely and swiftly terminated. The ball hit me right on the bridge of the nose. I fell to the turf in a lifeless lump, unable to see, as my eyes filled with tears. I gazed upward as my vision slowly cleared. I expected the concerned faces of my teammates. But the only face I saw belonged to my wife Lynne standing over me.

"Where are my teammates?" I mumbled.

"Your quarterback's mommy called; his dinner was ready. Billy starts junior high school tomorrow, and it's past his bedtime. Johnnie and Bobby said you were no fun to play with, and they took their football and went home. And, by the way, that was really a nice catch, dear."

I find it amazing how fragile manliness can be. One well-timed, sarcastic comment from virtually any woman can instantly strip away the thin veneer of any man's manliness.

Ma—Mother Of All Chickens

MA WAS THE SMALLEST OF A NINE-CHICK BROOD. SHE was also the most adventurous and daring.

Sister Patty had purchased a small clutch of chickens in hopes of establishing a direct source of deadly cholesterol in her own backyard. This is one of many stories concerning Ma, the infamous and fiendishly feathered fowl of the farmyard.

Ma established pecking order immediately. Though tiny in comparison to the other chicks, Ma assumed the role of sadistic guard in a chicken concentration camp.

Ma terrorized her brothers and sisters into sibling sub-mission by chasing them around the pen while pecking, pok-ing and pulling on their fuzzy little yellow heads.

One of the chicks was particularly frightened by Ma and would waddle away in sheer terror, peeping rapidly at about fifty decibels. Patty was to appropriately name that chick Peeping Tom.

Patty was basically a rookie chicken picker and had learned everything she didn't know about chickens from watching Ma and Pa Kettle in *The Egg and I.*

She had used large-mesh chicken wire to construct a good-sized chicken coop. The walls were high enough so that chicken-eatin' critters couldn't get in, but there was no roof to keep the chickens from getting out.

One day, while Peeping Tom was fleeing for his fowl existence, he ran right into the wire wall and, instead of bouncing off, he squirted right through.

Ma was relentless and quickly followed Tom to freedom. One after another, to Mother Hen's dismay, her chicks squeezed through the wire, scattering in all directions. Mother Hen, in a flying, feathered frenzy, flew up and over the roofless wire wall in pursuit of her babies.

It was early the next morning before the great escape was discovered. Patty found the remains of Mother Hen in front of a small, wooden, one-room house owned by the neighbor's dog. She spent hours looking for the chicks.

There were only two survivors. A loud, frightened squeal directed Patty to the underside of the hot tub where she found Ma engaged in a relentless attack on Peeping Tom.

Patty added numerous chickens over the years to her happy chicken family. Ma continued her terrorist ways. She was given the name Ma for her insistence on hatching and raising every chicken-child born in the pen. When eggs were laid, Ma would chase the egg layer away and sit on the eggs herself. She would hatch them and raise them as her own. The displaced mother chickens would often become sick with grief, but no chicken would challenge her authority. They were all a bunch of chickens, except one.

Patty had purchased a large hen that she named Amy Kay who immediately laid a nest full of eggs. There were ten in all. Ma tried to evict Amy Kay from her place on the eggs, but Amy Kay would have none of it. They were her eggs and she was gonna incubate 'em. Ma sat next to Amy Kay for three days and they fought. Beaks flashed and feathers flew but Amy Kay refused to budge. The noise and chicken chatter were incessant and unrelenting.

Patty awoke on the morning of the fourth day to an eerie silence. Had Ma finally won? Did Amy Kay survive? Patty rushed to the pen. Amy Kay and Ma sat there side by side. No flashing beaks and no flying feathers. Had Ma given up? Was Amy Kay the new queen of the roost? Patty lifted both birds gently from their nests. There were five eggs under each bird.

Patty never determined whether it was a fair and equitable compromise or just plain theft, but after the chicks were hatched, Ma, the infamous and fiendishly feathered fowl of the farmyard, stole all of the chicks away and raised them herself.

Ma, & The Younger Chicken

MA AND PEEPING TOM GREW VERY CLOSE AS THEY matured, though Tom remained quite hen-pecked. They were married on August 25, 1985. It was a quiet wedding, attended by a few close chickens, a horse, and the neighbor dog hoping for a stray wedding guest or two.

Most of the chickens refused to attend, not being particularly fond of Ma, the infamous and fiendishly feathered fowl of the farmyard.

Ma and Peeping Tom took a short honeymoon trip to the haystack next to the water trough. Ma, in apparent response to the lack of attendance at her nuptials, refused to roost in the pen with the other chickens. She would sleep on a limb of the apple tree with her main squeeze, Peeping Tom, who, as you may recall, suffered unmercifully at the beak of Ma during their youth, but was basically a loyal, clean, trustworthy kinda chicken. That is, until Red grew up.

Red was the finest looking little red hen Peeping Tom had ever set his eyes on. Neighboring roosters were known to have crowed at high noon after gettin' an eyeful of Red. Red was young and full of spunk. She would often strut her stuff

by swinging her tail feathers around the pen, scratching in the dirt while casting flirtatious glances and a flick of the beak in Tom's direction.

It wasn't long before Tom began looking at Ma with new eyes. Ma was a sturdy hen who had produced many a fine brood, but her beak was cracked in a couple of spots and she was getting a bit wide across the tail feathers. Peeping Tom was no spring chicken either but, as any middle-aged man can attest, it was difficult, if not completely impossible, for old Tom not to be flattered and totally self-absorbed by the fact that Red was attracted to what little was left of his roosterly prowess.

Soon Peeping Tom took to roosting next to Red, at first in private while Ma was nesting, and later in public for all to see. Ma was crushed. Had she finally met her match? Defeated, not in battle, but by the long, young, silken plumage of a red-feathered fowl, Ma began to withdraw from the other chickens. The mourning lasted three mornings. Ma would sit by herself in the corner of the pen and emit long soulful clucks. Was this the end of the infamous and fiendishly feathered fowl of the farmyard? Had the reign of Ma been cut short in its prime by the youth and beauty of a red-feathered hussy of a chicken?

At the crack of dawn on the fourth day of mourning, Ma could mourn no more. Ma was not the type of bird to take things sitting down. She was not a chicken that you wanted to rile. Hell hath no fury like a chicken scorned. Ma flew up to the branch where Red and Peeping Tom were sitting side by side and positioned herself on the other side of Tom. For three days Ma would reach around the back of Peeping Tom and peck Red upside the head. Then, by the fourth day, Red had suffered enough. She flew back to the pen and took up with a younger rooster. Peeping Tom, like any human male in the same predicament, was often observed regretting the entire incident.

Ma died in March of 1992 at the age of thirteen. I'm not sure if chickens normally live for thirteen years, but then I'm not really sure that Ma was a chicken. I know that Ma, the infamous and fiendishly feathered fowl of the farmyard, will be missed.

Beamin'

I BELIEVE THAT THE FICTION OF TODAY IS OFTEN THE basis for the reality of tomorrow. Not unlike *Star Trek*, I envision a future of rapid relocation via cellular disassembly, transportation, and reassembly.

I can envision an explosion of beaming terminology developed and perfected by none other than teenagers. Can't stay, man, gotta beam. Say man, beam me to the max. High beams, low beams, baked beams, beam bags, beam soup, string beams, bush beams, beamology and beamologists, jelly beams, and, yes, beamaholics who attend BA meetings (Beamaholics Anonymous).

I suspect that many of our country's youngest workers will become top-level managers for the DOB (Department of Beaming). The annual vacation would change significantly. Beaming would allow you to journey to a different exotic location every day and beam back home at night for a shower, hamburger, and a sip of drinkable water.

Travel agencies, set up similar to tanning salons, would offer Dream Beam vacations where you could pick a booth that was preset for a specific location, insert your master-beam charge card, and spend the day on an isolated beach on some South Pacific isle.

Companies would spring up all over the country, as PBBs (Personal Beaming Booths) become the hottest entertainment idea since eight-track tapes. Kids would be required to take beamer's education in high school, and beaming permits would net the government billions in license fees and taxes. People would be assigned beaming codes, and you could look up their beaming coordinates in the telebeam book.

The entertainment community would also chime in as new songs and plays on beaming flood the market with such artistic masterpieces as *A Midsummer's Night Beam* and *Beam a Little Beam for Me*.

There would, of course, be a down side to this new personal freedom. Companies would experience lost production and a significant increase in conduct-related problems as people are caught daybeaming during working hours.

Special "forbidden" beaming zones would have to be designated: such as banks, restrooms, and other people's houses. The new laws would require government hiring and training of beam patrols for enforcement and the issuance of beaming citations. Beaming accidents would become headline news as more and more people rush out to purchase personal beaming booths and a share of the great American beam.

Newspaper and television would flash the tragic stories of merged masses of beamed bodies as 453 Americans are killed or injured in beaming accidents over long holiday weekends, and sub-cultures would develop slang like "Totally bad beam, dude" for ill-chosen or errant-beaming destinations, such as 500 feet under water, inside solid rock, or in front of a 747 cruising at 38,000 feet.

The best part about the potential for future beaming is that most of us won't be here.

The Battle Of The Bedroom

MY WIFE AND I BOUGHT A HOUSE. MANY PEOPLE BUY houses. Buying a house is a significant piece of the American dream. Buying a house gives one a feeling of pride. Buying a house gives one a sense of well-being. Buying a house means that, in our society, you have achieved a level of affluence that is indicative of true success. Buying a house is often the culmination of all of our endeavors, and the ultimate realization of a lifelong dream.

But, mostly, buying a house is a big pain in the posterior. First, ya gotta find one. This is not as easy as it seems. To find a house, one must seek out the wisdom and assistance of somebody called a realtor. I'm not sure if these people are college graduates, retired federal employees, or con artists, but they are most definitely diplomats, bureaucrats, and politicians. I would recommend two days with a realtor as group therapy for anyone suffering from an inferiority complex.

The most important thing to consider when looking for a house is, of course, the wife. To a woman, the location of the house is paramount. It's gotta be close to schools, close to work, close to shopping, close to friends, but not too close to any neighbors. A man just needs to buy a house that he can find regularly without written directions.

Women are also incredible creatures of imagination. They can see things that aren't there—roses, flower beds, manicured lawns, rock walls and fruit trees. I see digging, mowing, pruning, hauling, lifting, watering and weeding. Women envision furniture layout, indoor plant placement, color schemes and curtain patterns. I see spackle spreading, sanding, wall building, furniture moving and painting.

I remember the battle of the bedroom. "I'll move our bed 'n' stuff in here tomorrow," I innocently commented.

Her response left little for discussion, "You can't move anything in here, you dummy. The walls need to be painted white!"

"But, my pet," I cowered, "the walls are white now."

"That's oyster white," she corrected. "Don't you know that I want *shell* white." I considered, for only a second, inquiring as to the difference between shell white, oyster white, and just plain old white, but I didn't make it this far by being a complete idiot.

I attempted to diffuse the situation with a rapid and gutless display of kowtowing. "I'll go ahead and paint it now, my pet."

"You can't start painting now," she instructed. "You have to spackle up the nail holes first." I was a spacklin' fool. I caught on to this spacklin' stuff immediately. You just gotta dip that old spackle knife in the can of spackle and lay a big glob of that stuff right over the hole. There were numerous holes, but I was done in fifteen minutes, and I only used up one pint of spackle.

I got up early the next morning, thinking I would sneak on over to the house and have that bedroom painted before the wife got up. I opened the paint, poured a sufficient amount in the roller tray, and grabbed a piece of sandpaper to remove the excess spackle from the walls. Wrong!

I can't find a way to make a thousand words do justice to the picture of my face when, after sanding the first hole for twenty minutes, I realized the magnitude of the task ahead. My arms ached. My fingers were raw from the sandpaper. I vowed to sand those big globs of spackle down and finish painting before she showed up and I would be forced to admit my stupidity. Not that she'd be surprised.

Two hours passed. Twelve spackle globs were smooth and flat. Twenty-one spackle globs remained. The paint in the roller tray had jelled. I audibly cursed the previous owner, though I knew it was probably his wife who had hung so many stupid pictures and knickknacks. I could sand no more. I was defeated.

The front door swung open, and I could hear her footsteps coming down the hallway. Closer and closer. "What are you doing, dear?" she inquired.

"I'm sanding down the spackle, my pet," I defensively responded.

"That's pretty dumb, dear," she chided. "That stuff comes right off with a sponge and a little water."

I find it amazing how fragile manliness can be. One well-timed, sarcastic comment from virtually any woman can instantly strip away the thin veneer of any man's manliness.

THE STAR SPACKLED BANTER

Oh, say, can you see
By the fifty-watt light
How profoundly I failed
'Cause the walls were not white.

Oh, say, does that jar
Spackled banter tirade
Over hand work by me
In the home of depraved.

Totally Pipeular

I WAS, ONCE AGAIN, IN THE WRONG LINE AT THE CAFE-
teria. There are two lines in the cafeteria: one line goes slow
and one line goes slower. After twenty years of working for
the same company, I haven't once selected the slow line. If
you see me in line at the cafeteria, immediately get in the
other line.

I paid for my fresh, handmade, taco salad, grabbed my
napkins and plastic utensils, and headed on back to the spot
I have occupied forever. I sat down in my chair. I know it's
my chair 'cause after twenty years it's starting to look like me
in a photographic-negative sort of way.

I am greeted by the fond, friendly, and familiar faces of
fraternal friends. Conversation is, of course, manly. "How
'bout them Seahawks?" "I rebuilt my four-cycle engine this
weekend." "Been doin' any fishin'?"

I was about to describe a recent battle with a man-eating
salmon when, out of the corner of my eye, I noticed a piece
of lettuce from my fresh, handmade, taco salad leap from my
plate. My eyes tightened into a semi-threatening, snake-like
squint.

"Yo! Which one of you guys threw something in my

fresh, handmade, taco salad?" My inquiry was greeted with numerous chuckles and then unanimous, straight-faced denial. I'm not sure why anyone would dare to mess with a guy that's built like me. Note: I must remember to work on my semi-threatening, snake-like squint.

Five minutes later I was in the middle of expressing my support for the quarter-backing skills of Joe Montana when, out of the same corner of the same eye, I noticed another piece of lettuce from my fresh, handmade, taco salad leap from my plate.

"Okay!" I yelled, patience growing thin. "Which one of you guys is throwing stuff in my salad?" Same chuckles, same denial, same lack of respect for my snake-like squint. "I'll ignore it," I thought to myself. "I'll ignore it. They won't get any response out of me, and they'll get bored and stop."

I was three bites shy of finishing my fresh, handmade, taco salad and listening intently to an exposé on the benefits of diesel-powered engines when, with everyone's hands in plain view, a piece of hamburger leaped from my plate. We all witnessed it. We all gazed at my plate, confused. The trajectory of the projectile was obvious. All heads, in unison, and as if attached to a common neck, slowly rotated upward.

There, from a four-inch-diameter pipe on the overhead, hung a solitary drop of liquid waiting for some unseen gravitational force to send it plummeting to my plate below.

What unpalatable substance was transported by the pipe? The source of the droplets was never determined. However, I am quite positive that potable water is not delivered in four-inch diameter, cast-iron pipes! I prefer to believe in the principles of condensation, but I've decided that it would be preferable, in this case, to remain ignorant.

As a precaution, if you ever observe me sitting in the cafeteria eating a fresh, handmade, taco salad, you would be well advised to sit elsewhere.

Murfsburra

THE YEAR WAS 1978 AND MY LIFELONG FRIEND JEFF
Tassin called me to say that he was getting married. Jeff is a
professional musician and was living in Nashville plying his
trade. He had been the best man at several of my weddings,
and he had called to request my presence at his side for his
upcoming nuptials. How could I refuse?

I was picked up by a mutual friend at the Nashville In-
ternational Airport several days before the big day, and I
moved into a spare room at his house.

Jeff had promised me a tour of Woodland Studio where
many famous country stars record. I arranged to meet Jeff in
downtown Nashville the next day on a street called Murfreesboro.

Nashville is a cultural contradiction. Walking a street
lined with three-story mansions—sporting pillars of white
marble framed by acres of manicured lawn—can rapidly, and
with little warning, lead you to row after row of crumbling
shacks. A Bremerton boy born and raised, I strolled, awe
struck, from affluence and prosperity to poverty and privation.
The heart of the Old South, I thought to myself, still beats.

I passed a river. I think it was a river. The water was

mud-puddle brown, and there was a noticeable absence of current. The street called Murfreesboro was nowhere to be found.

I noticed a small store set off about fifty feet from the side of the road, and I decided to stop in and ask for directions. The front of the store looked like a Norman Rockwell painting. There were two old rocking chairs—both occupied—and one of those old ten-cent Coke machines with the round top.

I strolled up to the porch to ask for directions. "Excuse me. Do any of you guys know where Murfreesboro is?" I found myself surrounded by half-a-dozen sets of glaring, bloodshot, good-ol'-boy eyes.

The reply was stern, cold and a good thirty seconds in coming. "Whatcha say, son?"

I suddenly felt somewhat ill at ease. My thoughts were dominated by the image from an old television commercial where the red-neck cop steps up to the car and says, "You're in a heap a trouble, boy."

I regained my composure, cleared my throat, and asked again. "I was wondering if any of you fine-looking and obviously extremely-educated gentlemen know where Murfreesboro is?" Silence.

Well, not total silence—I'm sure the whole town could hear my heart beat. I was mentally preparing to activate the one-hundred-eighty-degree turn with full-speed-retreat move when my mouth opened to speak all by itself.

"Did I mention that, in spite of his eventual, honorable, and dignified surrender, I have always considered Robert E. Lee to be the true hero of the Civil War?" I felt immediate empathy for every English-speaking comedian who has ever performed his entire one-hour routine in front of a non-English-speaking audience. It was the only time in my entire life that I had ever publicly threatened myself.

"Freeze!" I yelled, holding the tip of my ball-point pen to my temple. "Nobody move or the Yankee gets it!"

I wonder if, right before you actually lose your composure, your emotional status could be referred to as panic pending. It doesn't matter. I was saved, like in a B-movie, at the last minute. A tiny voice came from inside the store. "I think the boy means Murfsburra."

"Yeah, that's it," I stuttered. "Murfsburra."

I found out later that evening that I had three things going against me. I was a Yankee. I couldn't properly pronounce Murfsburra. And, only one kinda fella from up north says *guys.*

Nashville—Catfishin'

WELL, I FINALLY FOUND A STREET IN NASHVILLE CALLED Murfreesboro—pardon me, I mean Murfsburra. I met Jeff at the designated location and received my promised tour of Woodland Studio. Jeff introduced me to a guy named Benny.

Benny has led an interesting life. He used to know the road manager for Crosby, Stills and Nash. I guess that's like meeting, in person, the husband of the gal who makes some of the beds in the hotel where the bookkeeper of a famous person's assistant manager once slept. But, when names can be dropped, it doesn't make much sense to hang on to them.

Benny and I hit it off as soon as he mentioned fishing. I asked him what kind of wild, man-eating fish were caught around Nashville, and he said something about catfish.

"Benny, Benny, Benny," I ridiculed, "cats are not fish. Cats are arrogant, independent, furry, purry, lap-hugging, heat-leeches. Fish are silvery, streamlined, battlin' bundles of muscle-bound, scaly-armored, man-eatin' flesh."

Benny insisted that catfish fishin' can be fun and offered to take me that evening. He told me that catfish fishin' is something you do in the dark. I had to fly out early the next morning, but I always have time for fishin'.

"Sure, Benny," I patronized and condescended. "I'll go killer catfish fishin' with ya in the dark. What do ya use for bait? Catnip?"

I met Benny at nine o'clock that evening as planned. "Let's go purr-sue and cat-alog this purr-fect cat-egory of cat-aclysmic carp," I mumbled facetiously. Benny smiled. "Relax," he said. "We gotta juice up first." I told Benny that I would prefer not to drink and thanked him for the offer. Benny explained that the grasslands around Nashville are full of two types of skin-burrowing critters called ticks and chiggers, and to *juice-up* means to cover your entire body with a powerful smelling bug spray. We juiced up, grabbed the poles, and headed out the door.

I remember seeing my first lightning bugs as we pulled over and parked on the side of some old dirt road. Benny lit up a Coleman lantern, and we walked about two hundred yards down a path to a clearing. Benny hung the lantern from a tree branch and proudly exclaimed, "We're here. This is it."

"Where's the lake?" I asked.

Benny, obviously insulted, responded tersely, "What, you blind? That's it, right here in front of you!"

The only thing right in front of me was the biggest mud puddle I have ever seen. "Benny, Benny, Benny," I ridiculed, "this mudhole would be lucky to sustain a half-dozen, dirt-eating microbes."

Benny was not amused. "Here," he ordered, "put this on your hook." He handed me a one-inch-diameter ball of dough that smelled like it up and died three weeks ago.

"What's this?" I inquired, as my nose attempted to self-

seal.

"That's an aged cheese 'n' garlic bread ball," Benny explained. "It really stinks, but the catfish love it."

"I'm not surprised," I thought to myself, considering some of the places cats put their noses. I caught about a three-pound catfish that night. I was exhausted and not impressed. I promised Benny a real fishin' trip if he ever got up my way.

We got back to the house at about one o'clock in the
morning and I fell asleep standing up. At seven a.m., one
hour after the alarm was supposed to go off, I woke up. My
flight for Seattle was scheduled to depart in thirty-two minutes, and it was a good twenty-nine minutes to the airport. I
said some quick good-byes, grabbed my suitcase, and rushed
out the door.

In retrospect, I would give anything to have a picture of
the facial expressions of my fellow passengers. I don't think
even one of them bought my story about being a traveling
salesman for a new line of perspiration-seasoned, bug-spray-
flavored, aged garlic 'n' cheese doughball-scented after-shave.

Board Stiffs

SAILBOARDING IS A MANLY ENDEAVOR. MANLY SAIL-
boarding can only happen when real men manually hoist
their board, mast, and sail onto their broad and manly shoulders and defy death by sailing about on dangerous bodies of
water and facing ferocious man-killing winds. This is a story
about one such manly adventure.

Brother Jim and I were lounging around in lawn chairs
at his house on Tiger Lake. Smiles of satisfaction were etched
on our faces as we reminisced about our recent manly accom-
plishments. No words were spoken, but an understanding
glance and a nod of acknowledgment sealed our manly bond.

We had borrowed a sailboard from a mutual friend and
had spent the last several weeks participating in the manly
endeavor of learning the dangerous art of sailboarding.

A sailboard is, essentially, a tiny surf board with a big
mast and a huge sail. I remember the day we opened up the
package. "It's all in pieces," I mumbled. Jim glanced over at
me in a brotherly sort of way. "You know, bro," he said, "I sure
hope that your thought process isn't indicative of some kinda
genetic thing."

We laid the parts out on the lawn and discussed the

numerous possibilities for each cord, clip and fastener. "I think we should take the bottom part of this big stick-like thing and put it in one of these holes in the board," I offered.

"What if it's the wrong hole and the rope gadget doesn't thread through the plastic holder?" Jim responded.

This is the type of verbal exchange that stands as a typical representation of manly ingenuity.

Two hours passed. My wife Lynne watched the entire scene poised from her perch on the porch. I noticed her smirks and smiles and, in spite of my manly instincts, asked her what was on her mind. Her answer was, as usual, swift and merciless. "A woman, dear, would realize that there's no penalty for reading the instructions."

I find it amazing how fragile manliness can be. One well-timed, sarcastic comment from virtually any woman can instantly strip away the thin veneer of any man's manliness.

Lynne read the instructions while Jim and I assembled. We were finished in twenty minutes and ready for the first manly test.

There are few things manlier than riding out the violent thrusts of a surging sailboard. Time after time we mounted the board. Time after time a vicious three-knot wind would tear at the sail with the force of a full-blown hurricane and hurl our manly bodies, like rag dolls, into the cruel and unforgiving waters. Over and over again we pulled ourselves from the cold, wet depths of defeat and, as only men can do, climbed back on the surging bronco only to be cast again into the churning waves.

My wife, as a good wife should, offered her support from the dock. "You know, dear, that doesn't really look all that hard." I was instantly consumed by a manly surge of anger as my veins flushed with a flood of testosterone.

"Listen," I yelled, "this is an extraordinary physical challenge that requires the utmost balance and manly strength and spirit just to stay on!"

I regretted every word the second they left my lips, but the momentum of manly emotion often renders the male of the species hopelessly immobile with foot in mouth. Retribution for my *faux pas* was swift and, of course, ruthless, cruel, callous and heartless.

"You have a hard time staying on anything," she smirked. "I'm just surprised that your gut doesn't make a better counterbalance."

I find it amazing how fragile manliness can be. One well-timed, sarcastic comment from virtually any woman can instantly strip away the thin veneer of any man's manliness.

As the weeks wore on, our practice began to pay dividends. Soon we were sailing ten, twenty, even thirty yards at a time before crashing and cursing. We would travel hundreds of yards from the dock in the aforementioned increments only to discover that we lacked the necessary skills to turn around and come back. When we did master the turn, to our dismay the wind would die and we would sit stranded for unbearable lengths of time cursing Mother Nature for her audacity.

But, on this day, as I said earlier, smiles of satisfaction were etched on our faces. We both had sailed around the lake and back without getting wet, and we were able to comfortably exchange terms like *luffing* and *tacking* as expressions of our adeptness and as a basic means of satisfying the manly need to show off.

The sweet taste of a hard-won success cannot be described with mere words. Our moment of male bonding and silent satisfaction was poignant but short-lived.

It was interrupted by Lynne's loving voice. "Can I try that thing, sweetheart?" she asked innocently.

Jim and I exchanged smirks. "Sure, baby," I condescended, "but be real careful. It's a very dangerous sport."

Jim and I chuckled and watched as Lynne stepped on the board. She bent over, grabbed the rope, pulled up the mast, sailed around the lake twice, coasted back, stepped off the board right onto the dock without missing a beat, and walked directly to where Jim and I were sitting in stunned silence.

"You were right, dear," she smirked. "That was really, really tough."

I find it amazing how fragile manliness can be. One well-timed, sarcastic comment from virtually any woman can instantly strip away the thin veneer of any man's manliness.

Ballad Of The Bridge

THE SUN WAS PEEKING OVER THE SEATTLE SKYLINE ON A clear August morning in 1990. My wife Lynne, daughter Amberine, brother Jim and I had loaded our gear in friend Dale's boat for a day of salmon fishing off Port Angeles.

Dale is such a nice guy. I thought of him and his uncommon generosity as we prepared to begin our journey. His final words of support and comfort echoed in my brain: "You wreck my truck or my boat, Wilson, and you're dead meat!"

With that thought in mind, I decided to drive my car. I handed the truck keys to brother Jim and told him I'd be honored to let him drive Dale's vehicle. Brother Jim hopped in the truck, seat belt fastened, key turned, nothing, not even a click. Hood up, cables off, battery terminals cleaned and scraped, seat belt refastened, key turned, successful ignition, we were on our way.

I should have known right then.

We fished all day. The fishing was lousy, not even a nibble. The waves were six feet high. The sun was hot. We were freezing. The day was rapidly fading over the crest of the Olympics. Time to head home.

Lynne, Amberine and I led the procession across the

Hood Canal bridge. Brother Jim was behind in the truck. I lost sight of the truck in my rear view mirror, so I pulled over on the east side of the bridge and waited—ten seconds, thirty seconds, too long. I pulled a U-turn and headed back across the bridge.

There sat brother Jim. The truck was on the bridge, two-hundred yards from the end of it, with the hood up. I drove all the way back to the west side, turned around, and headed east again.

I pulled up behind the truck and hopped out. "What's wrong, bro?" I asked.

"The stupid thing just died!" he yelled. I climbed in the truck as brother Jim tweaked on the battery. She finally started. Brother Jim jumped in the passenger seat and yelled, "Let's get off the bridge!"

I hung my head out the window and told Lynne to drive the car over. When Jim and I reached the east side, we pulled over and waited—ten seconds, thirty seconds, too long. Red-faced, I found the car keys in my pocket. We were having fun now.

We pulled a U-turn. I jumped out when we reached the car, and brother Jim continued west across the bridge to turn around. I provided a rapid explanation to an extremely confused motorist who had stopped to help a poor stranded female, only to be told that she didn't have any keys.

After absorbing a violent verbal thrashing from Lynne, I drove the car to the east side of the bridge and waited—one minute, five minutes, too long! Another U-turn.

There was brother Jim two hundred yards from the west side of the bridge, out of gas! A one-hundred-twenty-dollar towing bill and two hours later we arrived home.

Clearwater Camping Caper

SUMMER 1983. DAVE AND I DECIDED TO TAKE THE KIDS camping. Why, oh why, would anyone in their right mind decide to take kids camping? I think it was my idea.

There we were—two dads, Dave's eight-year-old son, my thirteen-something-year-old daughter and her thirteen-something-year-old girl friend. Why, oh why, did we take the kids? I should have been shot for the thought.

Come to think of it, I almost was! I'll explain.

The Hoh Rain Forest lived up to its billing. Three observations come to mind: one-hundred-sixty inches of rain a year can actually happen in one day. Tenaciously dug, extra-wide, double-deep, around-the-tent drainage ditches are never tenaciously dug extra-wide or double-deep enough, and waterproof tents aren't.

We ate soggy pancakes with watered-down syrup for breakfast; played with soggy cards in a soggy tent; finally packed the soggy sleeping bags, soggy pillows, soggy kids and soggy tent into the back end of Dave's soggy station wagon; and loaded in our soggy bodies and headed home.

The kids whined about being cold, wet, hungry and car sick as soon as we left camp. "I gotta go to the bathroom."

"Are we home yet?" "Can I have a hamburger?" Why, oh why, would anyone in their right mind decide to take kids camping?

We took a shortcut past the Clearwater Corrections Facility. It would bring us out on Highway 101 somewhere around Third Beach. From there we could head south along the coast to home.

There was a sign about five miles before we got to the corrections facility that warned "No Stopping or Loitering for Five Miles."

"That's a funny sign," I thought out loud. "Why would anyone want to stop here anyway?" I suppose if I had said it to myself instead of aloud the car's engine wouldn't have heard me and sputtered to a stop. Dave pulled over, and we both got out and opened the hood.

"It's probably that black, round thing next to the little green piece of wire over there," I offered.

"Shut up and get the toolbox out of the trunk," Dave instructed.

As Dave screwed screws, bent bolts and crafted curses, a dark green truck pulled up twenty yards behind us. Two men got out and cautiously approached us from two different directions. Their hands were resting nervously on objects strapped to their belts.

"Yo, Da...Da...Dave," I stuttered.

"What now?" he yelled.

"These guys got guns," I mumbled.

"Sure they do," Dave calmly replied. "Don't worry about it. They can see we're campers."

Dave was probably right but I was wondering what we must look like from their point of view. Dave's long, blonde hair flowed down the back of his Harley Davidson leather jacket; I had a hunting knife strapped to my belt; I was wearing a ripped, soggy, flannel shirt; I hadn't shaved for a week; and we're sitting with the hood up less than two-hundred yards from the Clearwater Corrections Facility and right in front of that funny sign that said "No Stopping or Loitering for Five Miles."

I didn't have long to wonder. The tension was quickly broken by a loud, friendly greeting from the biggest guy, "Both of you back away from the car, slowly, with your hands in plain view!"

"This is it," I thought to myself. "I'm gonna die with Dave." The headlines in the morning paper will read, "Disaster Deals Death as Dad Dies with Dave."

Suddenly, from the back of the car came the sweetest sound I have ever heard and one I will never forget: "Are you done yet, Dad? I gotta go to the bathroom. Can we get some hamburgers?"

The guns were holstered, the two gentlemen helped us fix the car, and we continued on our way home. "You know, Dave," I proudly exclaimed, "it's a good thing I decided to bring the kids."

Jumping To Contusions

I HAVE HUNTED CABEZON AND LING COD IN THE COLD, murky depths below the surface of the Puget Sound.

I have stalked the killer steelhead trout and battled man-eating king salmon.

I have been strapped to Dale Fransen's circa 1976, nylon-covered, aluminum-framed, high-flying, tow-kite in a nerve-shattering flirtation with death.

I have crossed roaring rivers, danced with snakes, skipped across the open sea in a twelve-foot boat through six foot waves, and I have been married three times.

Yes, I have done all of these foolish things. I have pushed the outer boundaries of the envelope and I will push them further. I plan to witness someone, from the ground, of course, jump from an airplane in a free-falling gravitational plunge. I will observe others climb a sheer cliff of cold granite and see some poor soul single-handedly pilot a canoe down roaring, white-water rapids. Yes, I will watch all of these things and write about them in the first person.

What I will never, ever, do, under any circumstances, for any amount of money, even on a triple-double-dog dare, is let some bozo that I don't even know tie a flimsy, synthetic rubber band around my ankles and then tell me to go take a flying jump. I will not watch the ground, or the water, or concrete, or a pile of jagged rocks, or whatever, come toward my face at ninety miles an hour and offer to break my fall should the aforementioned flimsy rubber band fail to do so.

This mindless piece of insanity is currently in vogue and is referred to as bungy (bun-jee) jumping. They do it from hot-air balloons, overpasses, and railroad bridges high above roaring rivers. They do it in the wilderness, at air shows, and at county fairs. They do it for kicks, and they often travel long distances for the thrill of the dive. The most absurd aspect of this phenomena is the fact that they pay cold, hard cash for the opportunity.

My friend Duane, apparently, has no such fear. Duane may be a true para-dive pioneer or maybe a potential paralyzed pioneer. However, I personally feel that Duane is just plain nuts. Duane ventured to Canada last year and paid some entrepreneur one hundred bucks for the thrill of plunging through the air to his potential death. The jumping spot was a bridge that spanned a river gorge five hundred feet above the roaring, white water below.

Jumping from a bridge five-hundred feet above anything, roaring or unroaring, is impossible for me to comprehend. I have always had a very cautious and healthy respect for any height greater than three feet. I would have to slowly sneak up on the railing just to take a peek.

My arms would be stretched to maximum shoulder-joint socket tension. My knees would be bent to lower my center of gravity. And, my butt would be pointed backwards and

downwards in what would appear to be a feverish attempt to pull the rest of my body back to the safety of center span. When my hands finally did reach the railing, they would leave permanent fingerprint indentations.

I have found that once you have established your rail-bending death grip, the rest of your body contorts into some sort of ostrich-like creature, allowing your neck to stretch to unheard of lengths while your feet remain glued to one spot. This position enables your brain to view the abyss in small intervals, thus allowing for maximum control of your body's rate of adrenal release.

I have never been able to figure out why people, who profess to be your friends, inevitably take advantage of this vulnerable position by sneaking up behind you, digging their hands a good two inches into your rib cage, screaming some guttural death squeal, and then laughing hysterically as you grasp your heart in reflex anticipation of cardiac arrest.

Duane was asked to first stand on a scale to be weighed. The weight of the jumper, in conjunction with his height, is used to calculate the length of the bungy cord. This cipherin', as Jed Clampet used to say, is all accomplished by some guy that looks like he took high school remedial math and graduated in the lower half of his class.

The cord was tied around Duane's feet and he fearlessly stepped onto the platform. Duane exuded a cocky confidence. He looked down, took a deep breath, closed his eyes, leaned forward, and was rudely interrupted by a chuckling voice. "Hey, don't jump yet, partner. I ain't tied off the business end a this here cord yet."

Duane bent up and down at the waist like a chicken pickin' peanuts. His arms wildly mimicked a windmill as he struggled to reverse his forward momentum. Duane was infuriated. "What the heck are you trying to do, kill me?" he yelled.

"Don't yell at me!" the guy screamed back. "I got a heck of a hangover, and besides, it weren't me that paid money ta jump off this here bridge. 'Sides, I got li-bilty 'surance and we ain't lost but two people this month. How deep do ya figure ya wanna go anyways?" the voice inquired.

Duane's response, "What?" was immediate, and obviously intended to stun his new-found nemesis into providing pertinent information.

The man continued talking, apparently unaware of Duane's concern. "Well, ya see, we kin make this here rope long 'nough so's you kin stop before ya hit the water or we

can 'range it so ya go just about any ol' depth ya wanta go—
short a hittin' the bottom a the river, a course."

Now, like I said earlier, I feel that Duane is most likely
just plain nuts, but even nutty ol' Duane was wise enough to
conclude that an abort was in order. He bent down to remove

the cord from around his ankles, forgetting a primary rule of physics: A mass will react to the forces of gravity in a trajectory that is directly proportional to the distribution of weight. Over he went.

Townspeople ten miles away, upon hearing the ensuing high-pitched scream, were reported to have evacuated, assuming that the dam had broken and they were hearing the warning whistle. Fortunately, his nemesis was able to tie off the cord prior to Duane reaching the end of its length. Rumor has it that after plunging into the river below at nearly terminal velocity, the elasticity of the bungy cord, coupled with the sudden impact of his prone body and the added friction of the ice-cold water, halted Duane's descent slightly shy of the river bottom.

There was talk about him coming to the surface with three-inch-diameter eyeballs and a mouth full of gravel, but I didn't see it so you didn't hear it from me.

Now, if you were to ask Duane about this adventure, I'm sure he would tell you that his actions were intentional and his feat was truly manly. However, when you consider this author's well-documented and highly-reputed level of integrity, who ya gonna believe? Duane or me?

Things Are Looking Up

I WAS NINE YEARS OLD IN 1959. IT WAS THE ONLY TIME I can remember my father taking me camping without the rest of the family. I'm not sure where we were. I suppose it doesn't matter.

I do remember that it was by a river and that we were camped in the middle of a forest of giant trees. I remember lying by the fire as my father told me of the space satellite called Sputnik that the Russians had recently launched.

"Imagine," he said, "a small flying machine of metal and electronics circling the earth at speeds of over 17,000 miles per hour."

Remember that in 1959 the world was ten years away from men on the moon and several years away from men in space. I was fascinated by his description of such a magical thing.

I walked away from the fire where I could look up at the stars through a small clearing in the canopy of trees. There, appearing as a bright moving star across the tiny opening, was the satellite Sputnik. It was the only man-made object circling the earth in 1959, and I looked up through that tiny clearing and saw it pass.

The image is burned in my memory. The odds seem as infinite as the stars in the universe. Ever since that night, I have hunted satellites in the evening sky.

If you really want a truly manly adventure with no delusions, take your kids outside on a clear night, lie on the lawn, and gaze up at the stars. There, sometimes from two or three directions at once, sometimes faint and sometimes clear and bright, you will see the remnants of more than thirty years of space exploration.

You will not have to wait long. The sky is full of communication, weather and military satellites, spent rocket boosters, and assorted space junk. They appear as slightly wavy, slow-moving stars, due to a combination of atmospheric distortion, altitude, and the reflection of the sun off their metallic surfaces. Take a look and tell us what you see. Maybe, just maybe, you will see Sputnik.